YOUTUBE CHANNEL SUCCESS SECRETS FOR BEGINNERS 2020

The Ultimate Secrets to Building a Channel, Increase Views, Grow Your Following and Make Passive Income on YouTube as a Video Influencer

ANTHONY HENDERSON

Copyright

Anthony Henderson
ISBN: 9798649202763
ChurchGate Publishing House
USA | UK | Canada
© Churchgate Publishing House 2020

All rights reserved. No part of this publication may be reproduced, stored in a retrieval system or transmitted in any form or by any means, electronic, mechanical, photocopying, recording, and scanning without permission in writing by the author.

While the advice and information in this book are believed to be true and accurate at the date of publication, neither the authors nor the editors nor the publisher can accept any legal responsibility for any errors or omissions that may be made. The publisher makes no warranty, express or implied, with respect to the material contained herein.

Printed on acid-free paper.

Printed in the United States of America
© 2020 by Anthony Henderson

Table of Contents

Copyright i

Chapter 1 1

FEATURES AND IMPACT OF YOUTUBE 1

Impact of YouTube 8

The Ultimate Equipment Checklist On Becoming a Successful YouTuber 10

Audio Equipment Checklist 18

Tripod and Lightning Equipment Checklist 21

Secrets to Making Good Content on YouTube 24

Secrets to YouTube Algorithm most YouTubers Ignore 26

YouTube Tools to Help You Get Viewers 30

Steps to Making Your Video 35

Chapter 2 40

TIPS AND TRICKS TO YOUTUBE SEARCH ENGINE OPTIMIZATION 40

Techniques to Set up Thumbnails that Pops 48

Techniques to Drive Traffic to Your Youtube Channel You Must not Ignore 52

Techniques to take advantage of Youtube in the Business World 56

Steps to Broadcasting Live and Its Benefit 59

Promoting Your Merchandize on YouTube Channel . 62

Chapter 3 65

TIPS TO BE CONSISTENT ON YOUTUBE 65

YouTube Videos - Quality or Quantity 69

Steps to creating a YouTube AdSense account 70

YouTube Best Practices 73

Tips to make YouTube Videos go Viral Most YouTubers are not using 74

Setting up a YouTube channel for success: Things to take note of 77

YouTube Video Ideas and Crucial Things You Need to Know 84

Chapter 4 87

STEPS TO SHOOT A GOOD YOUTUBE VIDEO 87

YouTube Video structure 93

Structuring your video 94

YouTube Video Editing Tips and Tricks 97

The right ways to Upload Your Videos to YouTube . 100

Uploading a video to YouTube Using YouTube Account... 101

Tricks to Uploading YouTube videos through Screencast-O-Matic's Video platform 102

Tips for Maintaining YouTube followership............. 102

Ads for Monetizing YouTube Channel 105

About the Author 109

Chapter 1

FEATURES AND IMPACT OF YOUTUBE

Getting started on YouTube can be very scary, especially for small organizations and small scale businesses who are just exploring the platform. You also should know that no matter the tension and nervousness you might encounter while setting your YouTube channel, the benefit of being on YouTube greatly outweigh the downfall. Get over any impending obstacle that can mar you of owning your space.

One of the most important things you need for a successful YouTube channel is something you probably have known. Understanding the psychology of your audience is paramount by getting to know who they are and what they find valuable. For example, if you run a fashion store, you should know that your audiences are fashion lovers and find fashion-related tips, latest designs, and trends engaging.

Taking note of your audience, and their interest is quintessential in harnessing your focus when creating content for YouTube. Video content can reinforce your branding and put you at the acme of a stable fit by showing your business acumen and expertise.

However, it's also a great way to entertain, educate, and connect with people.

In a bid to truly make the best of this opportunity, here are the features of YouTube you should know while getting started.

1. YouTube Audio Library

Ever wondered after watching a YouTube video and left exclaimed about the super quality of the audio? Haven't you watched a YouTube video and made a verdict— it was the audio that created it? The emotional leaning evoked by music is un-debatable. Music has a way of evoking a strong emotional response in an audience. The right track has the power to elude a magical moment. You don't want to risk negotiating the goodwill of traffic you have by choosing bad audio while putting together successive content. Finding the right music for a video is a daunting challenge, especially when you are on a budget.

How do you select a music track?

- Get the YouTube Audio Library via the creation Tool menu in the Video Manager section of your YouTube account.
- Filter the list by genre, mood, instrument or duration
- Preview the track.
- Click on the download icon when you find the perfect song.

2. YouTube Fan Finder

Ever thought of YouTube offering you ad space on its website targeting people who would find your content engaging? Well, you get no worries. That's the job of Fan Finder.

How does it work?

The YouTube Fan Finder program intimates you of submitting up to five "channel ads." These ads will target people that the site believes would love your content. Channel ads are short video contents that show off your brand in a bid to get viewers' attention by telling them about you and the need to check you out.

Getting started

- Upload a channel ad as if it were an ordinary video
- Submit it for review through the Fan Finder page
- Click your Channel ad button
- Select a video you want to use.

Note:

YouTube recommends that you keep your channel ad short and engaging. Deploy clear and repeat branding so that viewers can remember you Communicate in a concise version, what your channel is all about and ingrained a clear call for action. It's safe to introduce yourself to people who might not have known you before while grabbing their attention in the next 5seconds.

3. Associated Website Annotation

Do you know you can insert a call to action together with a link to a website in a YouTube video content? Using an annotation within the video player itself, you can also add a clickable link to your chosen website. This can be done using associated website annotation.

How?

- Ascertain the ownership of your YouTube account through a quick two-step telephone process at https://www.youtube.com/verify.
- Add your website as an associated website in Google Webmaster Tool.
- Finalize a second short verification to confirm that the domain belongs to you before you link it to your YouTube account
- Go to the Advanced Section of the Channel Setting menu of your YouTube account
- Input your website URL to the box next to the associated website
- A green success circle will be displayed if everything went perfect
- You now can add a clickable link directly to that URL within a video

4. **InVideo Programming**

In building traffic, one of the steps you would want to take is to find a way of keeping viewers, who hitherto had watched your content, keep watching following materials. Create a strong brand identity in consonant with a constant stream of fascinating content. InVideo Programming reinforces channel branding and drives viewers. With InVideo Programming, you can infuse a clickable thumbnail of your channel, logo or video across all videos on your YouTube channel.

Getting Started

- Go to the video manager page
- Select InVideo Programming from the channel setting menu
- Upload a video to display over a video/videos you want viewers to see
- In case of a watermark, use a transparent image with a single color
- You can add a featured video by accompanying it with a caption and persuade viewers to click and check it out.
- You can decide when the image would appear. At the start, end or for a custom duration within your videos.

Impact of YouTube

This is an attempt to examine the output of colossal video output. While I will be relaying the positive effect and then following it by a negative impact, you can counter every positive with a negative.

- **YouTube makes us smarter.**

There is a video for everything. Need to fix your gadget? You can learn how to do it in a matter of minutes. You can be a professional in Digital marketing by watching videos on YouTube. Just lay your hands on few videos and you are good.

- **Getting misinformed with YouTube videos and not even aware**

Just that a video exists doesn't make it the absolute truth. It also doesn't set free, the person teaching the video as an expert, and indeed, there is no assurance that you will get what is being conveyed perfectly. Unlike a TV show or radio presentation that requires people vetting, a random person says a boy of 13 can launch a channel without any scrutiny. This makes YouTube quite vulnerable.

- **YouTube Streaming cost you money.**

Live streaming YouTube's video costs money, maybe inform of data consumption or clicking on ads. Even if you don't acknowledge the ads, the video you are watching might still intimate for you, a kind of advertisement or product placement.

- **YouTube leads to less boredom.**

With your mobile device, you can enjoy vast videos that are on YouTube. Just your Wi-Fi connection, you are good to go. It's such in handy that you can enjoy your video on your mobile device any day, any time. At a car park, on an airplane, at work and during leisure hours. When you are bored, just take to YouTube.

- **YouTube has led to the creation of many jobs and income**

From the onset, YouTube started as a platform where people can upload videos they captured. Now, people are dedicating their time to creating useful content. We now have professionals. YouTube personality is a full-time job for some people and a part-time gig for many, while YouTube compensates them for their services. The onus is the creative economy has opened a world of opportunity for many to earn income.

The Ultimate Equipment Checklist On Becoming a Successful YouTuber

Venturing into YouTube production doubled as taking a juicy career and making cool cash. What do you do? Simple! You find a gap (a problem), you leverage on the gap by bridging the gap and making money out of it— you create a video that solves a specific issue. Sounds interesting, right? Let's dive into the nitty-gritty of becoming a successful YouTuber.

Of the thousands of YouTubers that you see out there, a sizable number of them have created a solid niche that can stand the test of time. Every market and enterprise you see is massively competitive. If you want to enlist the few eagle-eyed gurus that have created a solid seat comes stormy days, then you need to know the art before you explore the craft. A long journey of struggle, hard work, and investment are processes you must acknowledge and more before you create a YouTube video. This e-book is a juicy and ultimate checklist that is written to bring fortunes and ease your random searches about creating your YouTube video. Won't you rather dine?

- Assessing your equipment: The essential nature of oxygen to human existence can be likened to the inevitability of equipment type in making a successful YouTube video.

The following are the ultimate equipment checklist in becoming a successful YouTuber;

- o Camera equipment for YouTube
- o Audio equipment for YouTube
- o Tripod and Lighting equipment for YouTube

- **Camera equipment for YouTube**

If your dream is to become a YouTube superstar, you must invest in quality cameras for shooting videos. The reason isn't farfetched. Several persons want video footage to be either in full HD or 4k. The ability of the viewers to see everything that you are saying in a video is an excellent selling point. Leverage on that in creating your first impression. While there are many pieces of equipment in shooting a YouTube video, a camera is an essential equipment you don't want to joke with. If you fine-tune your video's aesthetic through a juicy camera, you are one way up to your A-game. The following are the camera type you will want to consider;

- Cell phone
- Webcam
- Camcorder
- Action camera
- DSLR

Cell phone

While you are still an absolute beginner and you are eyeing a spot in becoming one of the best YouTubers, you can use your cell phone camera to shoot video. The advantage of this is that it's pocket friendly. Here, several users have an individual likeness for the selfie camera. You can go for the primary camera, which is much more powerful. The cell phone camera helps you create content on a mild budget. With time, you can upgrade your camera from a cellphone to more sophisticated ones.

Webcam

As a beginner looking for an affordable setup for YouTube videos, a webcam is one of the many places to start. With a webcam, videos with not much production value can be implemented. A good webcam is the Logitech HD Pro C920. With this, you can initiate your video shooting at your desk, company meetings, and execute live stream Q and A. A webcam is mostly recommended for live streaming over any other camera since they are connected directly to a computer. The Logitech HD Pro C920 offers a full HD video recording. It has 1920 by 1080 resolution with an automatic low light correction. It has a dual stereo microphone too. To complete your work, all you need is a laptop (window 7) with a USB port. The device is so flexible with a universal clip that fits all monitors. Other webcam options include; Logitech C310, Logitech Streamcam, and Razer Kiyo.

Logitech HD Pro C920

Camcorder

One of the best options for creating YouTube content is the camcorder. Specifically, they are configured to record video. There has been an increase in the grades of camcorders over the years. The most recent Camcorders are light weighted, compact, and affordable. Of course, camcorders are not the only choice of videographers. The best 4k cameras for filmmaking does not only provide gorgeous pictures but also offers users the capacity to swap lenses. The Sony FDR AX-33 is a portable and affordable fantastic 4k camcorder with the following properties; Light and compact, 3840 by 2160px, Image sensor: Exmor R

CMOS sensor, Total pixel: 8.29MP, No HDR, 5.1 channel microphone.

Other camcorder types include; Panasonic HC-X1000e, Sony FDR-AX700, Canon XA 40 and Sony HDRCX405.

Sony FDR AX-33

Action camera

Of all camera types, action cameras have the most versatile and compact features. They are best for videographers who have a unique likeness for sporting adventures. Though they are small, they can produce the best quality video. This is why a survey of YouTubers use action cameras for the video quality and durability they have. The best action camera you should consider is the GoPro HERO8 Black. It has several features ranging from 4k video at 60fps, waterproof without a case, built-in mounting system, super image stabilization, and screen smaller than DJI. Other action cameras include; GoPro Hero7 Black, DJI Osmo action, Yi 4k+ Action camera, and Sony RXO mark II.

GoPro HERO8 Black

DSLR

For their high-quality result, DSLRs have an edge among YouTubers. The ability to adapt in a dim-lighted environment and sparking video quality are some of the reasons why they are an excellent choice for creating YouTube content. Picking the best DSLR camera is quite a daunting task. However, the needs vary according to customer's demand. For a beginner, laying hands on a top-spec high-level DSLR makes no sense as well as a professional looking for an entry-level DSLR camera type. In a bid to play safe, you will want to sit in the middle of the two extremes. Nikon D850 is the best DSLR camera known. As a beginner, you will want to consider the Nikon D3500. It has several useful features; Terrific 24MP sensor, Excellent value for money, Basic external control, only 1080P HD video, and Beginner's friendly.

Nikon D3500

Audio Equipment Checklist

To have a compelling YouTube video, you want to compliment a quality video with excellent sound quality. Content with the highest possible video but with a dull audio quality will mostly keep viewers off within a few moments of exploring your channel. Camera microphones and built-in laptops usually have bad audio quality as they are unable to effectively record low sounds. To nip in the bud, this problem, you are to adopt a good quality microphone. The following are the list of available microphones to compensate for a quality video output you have shot;

- USB microphone
- Condenser microphone
- Lapel microphone

USB microphone

In recent times, the USB microphone is one of the best equipment YouTubers explore. The microphone has created an incredible niche for itself due to the sound quality it offers and usage flexibility. Their affordability and versatility are an added advantage. The Logitech H540 wired headset is a fantastic microphone headset for YouTube video making. As a USB mic-headset, you can begin recording once plugged into your computer.

Logitech H540 Wired headset

Condenser Microphone

The advantage of this type of microphone is that they allow for self-monitoring through its built-in headphone jack with volume control. Condenser microphone provides for the mixing of pre-recorded audio with microphone audio. An excellent example of condenser you may want to consider is AT5047, which captures the full, expressive character of a sound source. It is incorporated with a transformer-coupled output. The microphone maintains a stable load output impedance.

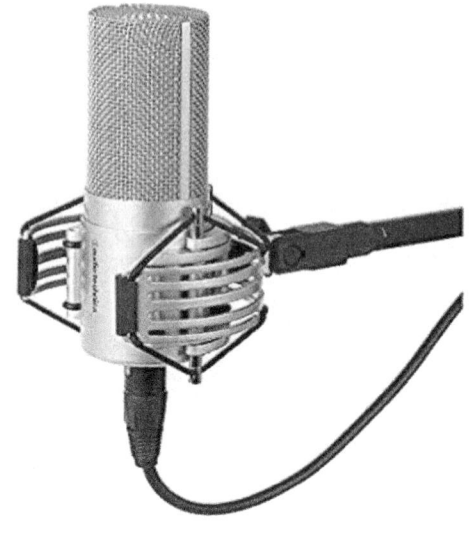

AT5047

Lapel Microphone

Lapel Microphones are popularly known as lapel Mic. They are small and can be attached to the shirt, collar, or tie. One of the most significant advantages of lapel Mic is that they allow for hands-free recording. All you need is to position it correctly, and you are set for work. They are great for videos and are mostly used with iPhones and cameras because of their unobtrusive nature. Lapel microphones are wireless, while some are made with wire. While there are a range of lapel microphone, RodeLink filmmaker kit is one you will have a pleasant experience with, both as a beginner and an expert YouTuber. It had a frequency of 2.4GHz, looks excellent, and has a button pairing. Other lapel mic includes; RodeLink Digital Wireless system, Sennheiser XSW-D Portable Lavalier Set, Saramonic Dual Wireless Lavalier Microphone Bundle and Sennheiser AVX – MKE2 Lavalier Pro Set.

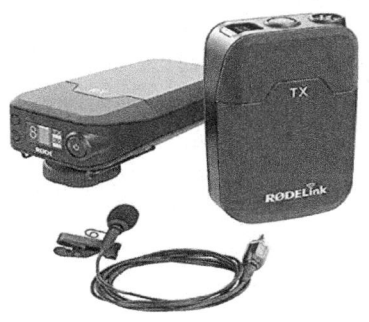

RodeLink filmmaker kit

Tripod and Lightning Equipment Checklist

Tripod

The importance of investing in sturdier, more reliable tripod can't be overemphasized to ensure the safety of your camera. The ikan E-image EGO1A2 is a low-cost super quality tripod and can handle most camcorders. It's capable of extending its leg higher than 5 feet. It's handy and compact— hence, you can shoot from any desirable point.

Lighting

Lighting equipment becomes the most sought when your shootings are mostly done indoors and in areas with low light concentration. On-camera lighting is one of the best lighting equipment.

- On-camera lighting

This camera type provides incessant lighting and can be incorporated on camera by mounting. It's deployed for YouTube content that involves people and dimly-lit locations. It is used in video content, capturing documentary and wedding. The ikan ILED-MA Micro Flood Light is a juicy choice for indoor shooting. It has a wide 120-degree beam of bright 5000k +daylight. It's chargeable with a MicroUSB cable and can be positioned vertically and horizontally on cameras.

ikan ILED-MA Micro Flood Light

Video editing software

For post-production, you will have to look for good video editing software. This stage will come after all the hardware has been set. YouTube has video editing software, but you should have your video software to modify your video all you want.

Secrets to Making Good Content on YouTube

The ability to hold attention is far better than getting the attention of someone. This is the fundamental principle in creating a niche for oneself for a booming YouTube career. A video that keeps viewers watching in recurring terms will be ranked higher over those that attracted few clicks. This shouldn't be the only motivator that pushes people in creating a high-quality output but also aligned with Erics Meyerson's view when he opined; it's in alignment with YouTube's goal to become the most essential media in people's life.

How can a YouTuber leverage on quality content in earning an incredible badge and gain higher ranking with YouTube ever-increasing algorithms?

The following are ways to achieve that;

- **Know your audience**

Audiences are the final consumer of your content. Hence, the need for you to research your audience. Don't assume you know them. What do they want? How old are they? What are their hobbies? What tends to keep them off the radar? These are essential questions that must be factored into the scheme of things while setting out.

- **Plan Ahead Pre-production**

You don't dish out content impromptu and expect an output that would worth the clap. Quality videos don't happen perchance. Deliberate efforts make them. They are created with pre-production planning. The following should be considered;

- Highlight and list all the shots you need
- Draw out a simple drawing of any complex transition
- Consider additional footage that would make your story come to life during editing
- Be energetic.

One of the qualities that could mesmerize and hypnotize your audience is the ability to exude passion coupled with energy while discharging content. This is a way safer than people who are drab and dull-looking during content discharge.

- Take Risk

Once you understand your audience's psychology, you trust your gut and take a calculated risk. While there are several untested assumptions, don't be timid in putting common beliefs into a test.

- **Pay attention to the description.**

Use Google keyword's tool to know if your word selection is popular. This would come as a rescue when a hitherto engaging YouTube video suddenly pushes viewers off due to poor choice of words in your headline.

Secrets to YouTube Algorithm most YouTubers Ignore

Every minute, over 400hours of video content is uploaded on YouTube. YouTube audience and content creators are growing at an astronomical pace. In such a massively competitive atmosphere, standing differrence among the oceanic volume of crowds might be daunting a challenge. Luckily, YouTube's algorithm is creating an equal-level plane for all content creators. Until recently, the YouTube channel's authority maintained that the number of views, subscribers, and watch time were vital ranking factors for the algorithm. The narrative is different now. YouTube's algorithm is moving away from this model. YouTube algorithm is a medium that renders the most personalized content to its user. There are five differrent sections where a video can appear on YouTube viz;

- Search
- Home
- Suggested videos
- Trending
- Subscription

Each of these sections would be simplified as follows.

- **Search**

YouTube is the second largest search engine. One of YouTube's goals is to provide answers to the user's query. The ranking of videos are based on several factors ranging from how well -the title, video content, and description - matches the viewer's question.

How do you leverage the search section?

- Ensure all the metadata of a video accurately describes the video content.
- Ensure to optimize Titles, Descriptions, Tags, and close captions.
- Ensure your video has a customized thumbnail
- Adopt a crisp and short title.

- **Suggested Videos**

These are potential videos that a viewer might be interested in watching. This is as a result of their past YouTube activities. There are pointers YouTube uses while giving suggestions on which video to be suggested. YouTube leverage on;

- Videos watched by viewers along with the current video they are watching.
- Videos that are topically rated.
- Videos from previous watch history of viewers.

How do you cash in on the suggested videos?

Ensure you include the important keyword or keyword phrase relevant to the content you dish out in your YouTube tag.

- **Home**

The first page that pops up when you open the YouTube app or visit the official YouTube site is the home page. The advantage of the home is that your videos can be accessible to non-subscribers.

How do you take advantage of this?

- Ensure to keep your tag broad as much as possible to carve a wide range for potential viewers
- Adopt a single-word relevant tag to maximize your reach
-

- **Subscribers**

People who have subscribed to be consuming your content are known as subscribers. These people must have subscribed due to a number of factors that can be referred generally to as your unique selling point. The frequency of your content can be adjusted in the YouTube setting. Your subscribers can see your new content in the subscribe tab.

How do you utilize this to your gain?

Always reinforce a call to action by intimating your audience to subscribe to your channel at the beginning of your content presentation or at specific intervals

- **Trending**

The trending contains an assemblage of popular videos in a viewer's country of residence. YouTube explores the geography where the video is coming from to feature it on trending. It is very pertinent to state here that YouTube places great importance on the growth rate of reviews rather than the cumulative number of views to be on trending.

How to take advantage of trending?

- Never stop producing high-quality contents
- Never stop engaging with your audience
- Advertise and promote your channel in media platforms

YouTube Tools to Help You Get Viewers

The need for personal branding isn't alien to the 21st-century small scale enterprise, companies, and big organizations. YouTube is one of the most popular websites in the world. It offers a gamut of opportunities for marketers and businesses to reach their target audience with compelling topnotch content. Ever wondered how you can leverage this juicy platform to its peak by growing your channel and gaining more viewers? You are in the right place. The following are YouTube tools for managing your channel and growing more viewers;

- TubeBuddy
- VidIQ
- Camtasia
- Social Blade
- YouTube Studio
- Woobox
-

TubeBuddy

One advantage of the TubeBuddy is that it's a free browser extension, as opposed to other software that you will download and explore separately each time you want to cash in on its features.

TubeBuddy automatically incorporates your YouTube and help you manage your channel. TubeBuddy gives you the luxury to execute tests that would advance the performance of your content.

You actually can test;
- Tags
- Descriptions
- Thumbnails
- Titles

This tool will assist you in finding which of these features work best for your channel. TubeBuddy monitors your ranking and compares with those of your competitor on YouTube and Google searches. With TubeBuddy, you can upload hundreds of videos at a time. With this tool, you can actually improve your thumbnail creation process.

One striking advantage of TubeBuddy is that it has several options for different categories of YouTube users, such as bands, networks, agencies, and creators.

vidIQ

Plus other tracking tools, vidIQ, also helps to monitor and track your YouTube audio analysis. When you get to know who consumes your content, understand their psychology, leverage on it, and create successive videos accordingly. Detailed reports of your YouTube channel can be obtained with vidIQ while also offering SEO tools. One of the key advantages of vidIQ is that you can identify influencers, manage comments, and run a high competitive comparison against other in-demand channels. Your engagement metric both on YouTube and Facebook can be tracked.

Camtasia

This is an excellent tool for screen recording and video editor. One of the ways to enhance your content is screen recording. It's inefficient and unprofessional to record your screen with a camera or Smartphone. When you finished recording your screen, you can mark up the video, edit, and add effects. In Camtasia, a voice narration features give you the autonomy to record yourself speaking or after the screen might have been recorded. Camtasia has an audio effect and has the option to add music.

Social Blade

A survey of options you may want to explore in a bid to upsurge the number of viewers on your channel, Social Blade, is an incredibly good option. With different statistics, it tracks on YouTube, Instagram, and Twitter. In terms of social media marketing strategy, Social Blade has got you covered. It also gives you an avenue to track your statistics and those of your competitors. You actually can compare up to three channels at a time giving you cliche on how you can be up to your game. The most exciting advantage of the Social Blade is that it offers a tutorial for beginners and long-term YouTube creators.

YouTube Studio

This is the official YouTube app for creators. On the go, you can manage your channel on your mobile device with YouTube Studio. This would mean that you can actually do without a computer anytime you want to handle something on your page. Just like every other tool, YouTube Studio allows users to monitor the performance of their channel. With the tool, users have control over monetization setting, thumbnails, scheduling and other settings from the app.

Woobox

Ever thought of promoting your channel on other channels? Woobox is a perfect tool for you. Social media is a platform you can use to re-negotiate your video content. Woobox allows you to set up your YouTube video on the Facebook tab. An excellent way for you to get more subscribers is to woodbox those you eventually would turn to customers.

Steps to Making Your Video

In a bid to create your first video as a beginner, there are several factors you must consider while putting things together.

The following are guides to making your YouTube video;
- Plan your video
- Prepare your equipment
- Set the stage
- Prepare yourself to be on camera.

- Hit record
- Edit your work
- **Plan Your Video**

The first question you should ask yourself is, why are you creating this video? The content of your video should fall within these categories base on popular demand; Education, Engagement, and Awareness.

When you are aware of your video's content, an actionable plan on how you are going to do it becomes less tricky. This plan will incorporate everything you need to create your video. You thought of adding a script afterward, you should plan it together. In the grand scheme of things, this plan will make life easier for you by ten folds.

When you are stuck and unsure of how to create a YouTube video, try answering the following questions, and you are on a safe radar. The items are as follows;
- What message will by video pass across?
- Who are my target audiences?
- Do I have a budget?
- How many people do I need?
- What is the target length?

- Where will the video be shot?
- Will there be speaking in the video?
- Will I need a script?
- What equipment do I have?

Answering these questions should ease the tension you might hitherto have had.

- **Prepare your equipment**

After you have perfected your plan, the next phase is the execution of your project. Different video content requires quite different equipment. You should consider your budget too in choosing your equipment. To create your video, you will need the following; Camera, Microphone, Lighting, Storage, Editing software.

- **Set the stage**

In making a YouTube video, you need to set the stage. What this connotes is that you are preparing a place you are going to record as to look best on camera.

In recording an entertainment Vlog, this would mean choosing a spot in a room with the beat lighting and creating a background that suits.

- **Prepare yourself to be on camera**

Being on camera can be scary, but this is a minus to the quality of your content should you be swayed by it. You can overcome this and make it look exciting for yourself and, most importantly, your viewers. One way of making the best in preparing yourself on camera is to see the camera as someone to strike a conversation with. See it as one of your audience and talk directly to them. Be energetic, smile, and stick to the topic.

- **Hit Record**

Having followed the steps above, it's time to turn your camera on and hit record! Always keep the following in mind no matter what you are recording;
- Keep the camera rolling
- When you make a mistake, don't start over. Take it shortly from where you make a mistake and redress it without turning off your camera. You can always fix the rest during editing.
- Acknowledge what you don't know

- **Editing your work**

When you are done putting your video together, it's time to edit your work. Here, you clean up the mistakes you have made while perfecting the video to go online.

During editing, remember you;

Put your scenes or place it in the right order

Remove unwanted footage

Software equipment is one of the investments you would want to consider. It has the power to super change what you have created on YouTube and turn it into video worth pro.

Chapter 2

TIPS AND TRICKS TO YOUTUBE SEARCH ENGINE OPTIMIZATION

Search engine optimization (SEO) is the ever-dynamic practice of designing web content that could find a space in the ranking of search engine results pages. Search is often the most significant route to your materials. Optimizing your website to better position it for search is inevitable as this would attract you enormous traffic with a consequent surge in following. YouTube SEO deals with optimizing your metadata, channels, playlist, description, and the video them-selves. One crucial component about YouTube SEO is harnessing your video text's power in the form of transcripts, subtitles, and closed captions.

The following are the secrets to maximizing views and increasing your search rank;

1. **Lose your YouTube ASR Captions and Add Accurate Close Captions:**
YouTube now automatically transcribes videos. However, YouTube auto-captions are 70% accurate, which can make frustrating and embarrassing cap-tions. If you adopt YouTube auto-caption, you risk being labeled a spam and stand a chance of losing search ranking for your channel. How do you nip in the bud, this harmful effect? You must adopt closed

captions for your YouTube channel. The transcript of your video should contain the relevant keyword that describes your video content. Since search engines can crawl text, your transcript can be ranked accordingly. It's very imperative to note that there are a couple of transcription option which are cheap but time-consuming. The smartest way you would want to adopt is to send your video to a professional video transcription service. Professional video services are of high quality with little return time.

The benefit of closed caption
- YouTube videos with close captions have increased user engagement, which results in a higher search rank.
- With the closed caption, your YouTube video becomes more accessible to viewers who have a hearing impairment.
- People can watch your video in a noisy environment or a calm atmosphere with the audio muted.

2. Ensure you add a transcript to the video description:

Ever thought of which best approach you could adopt for displaying your video content on YouTube in the text? A video description is an excellent option for displaying your transcript on YouTube. Do you know that the description field contains 4,850 characters, including spaces? This is a perfect corner for scribing a 10minutes robust dialogue. The video description is a sharp spot for search engines to crawl your texts. If your transcript is ingrained with keywords from your video content, it's an excellent thumb up for YouTube SEO. Blogs, infographics, whitepapers, fact sheets, and website copy are great uses of video transcript. In a nutshell, incorporate video transcript as part of your strategy for SEO optimization.

3. Ensure you translate your video transcript and do subtitle in multiple languages:

Leaving your transcript subtitled in multiple languages would mean increasing the potential of viewers. The message you are passing can reach non-English native speakers when you subtitle your videos in diverse styles. This is a considerable chance for YouTube SEO;

hence, you stand a high ranking for non-English keywords due to mild competition.

4. **Type a keyword, optimized title, descript-ion, and tags:**
Going further, keywords and keyword phrases should match with; What describes your video perfectly, the words and group of words users input in search engine fields to find content like yours. For example, if you publish a video on "How to order a product on amazon," make sure you optimize your title, descriptions, and tag for "How to order a product on amazon."

To be at par with people's needs, use YouTube analytics tools to find which keyword people use when typing on search engines. You can leverage the keyword most used for your targeted audience. Also, it's essential to look for keywords variation. This will give you time to choose from less competitive options. After you might have chosen your keyword, incurporate them into the following fields;

- Title: The maximum character here is 100. Why not truncate it at 66 characters? You want to ensure that your most important information is within reach. Occupying the whole 100 characters would give space for much description, a probable minus to your gigs. Rather, use compelling language that would hypnotize the potential audience to click: words like "how-to," "advice," "tips," or a numbered list.

- Meta-description: Maximum characters are 5000. You want to truncate at 166 characters. A link to your product is an added advantage for eCommerce websites. Always include http:// to make your link clickable.
- Tags: These fit for 120 maximum characters. Ensure you adopt quotes (") to wrap phrases. For example, you should tag your video as "how to order a product on amazon" not "how to order product" on "amazon." It's safe to always think like a user and add tags in order of importance.

NOTE: If you will be posting your videos on a survey of platform aside YouTube, ensure you vary the keyword a bit. You don't want to compete against yourself.

5. **Pronounce your target keyword in your video:**
After you must have synthesized a perfect keyword, you should feature it in your title, tags, description, and transcript. With your transcript and captions, YouTube ranks your videos accordingly. You can use the YouTube search suggest to look for an appropriate keyword for your video in case you are blank.

6. **Adopt a compelling thumbnail:**
YouTubers can decide which frame to display as the video thumbnail. YouTube usually presents several screenshots to choose from, but you have the chance to upload your image either. When you choose the right video thumbnail image, there is a surge in the click-through rate. Remember that a high-quality contrast image works perfectly. Ideally, you want an image that represents and display your keyword. This will take your search results a bit ahead.

7. **Make use of the video SEO embed**:
For your video to have the competitive edge of being prioritized by Google, it must have suitable metadata. What the SEO embed does is that it ingrain all your

video metadata say your tags, description, transcript, and thumbnail to the top of your page for Google to crawl and index your video well. You get 2-5times more views when you optimize your video for Google than optimizing for YouTube alone.

8. **Focus on user engagement:**
How users respond to your content matters to Google since that's what keeps people glue to their site of preference. The following are variables to consider;

9. **Watch time:**
This is the actual time spent watching a video. For example, a 45% completion of a 15minutes video would rank higher than 100%completion of a 5minutes video. It's pertinent to mesmerize your viewers within the first 15 seconds with a teaser.

10. **Session watch time:**
Another user engagement technique is the session watch time. YouTube places much importance on how a video contributes to the user's overall viewing session. YouTube wants users to spend more time on their platform and tends to favor such videos that made them achieve that goal.

11. **The intent of users:**
Google can't read your mind, but Google can decipher what searchers mean. For example, if you are to type "how to create an ad on YouTube," you will be shown a video on "how to market your product through ads." When creating a title for your video, ensure you adopt keywords that are compelling and relevant.

12. **The playlist of users:**
A concise, relevant, and subcategorized playlist can significantly influence your engagement. It also makes it possible to share multiple videos per time.

Techniques to Set up Thumbnails that Pops

A thumbnail is the first impression of your video. A dull first impression could mean a turn off for your potential viewers. Thumbnail is the face of your video, and it's one that reaches your audience first. You must be sure whether your thumbnail portrays the content of your video. What this means is that your thumbnail must mirror your video, has captivating visuals, well branded, simple and basic, original, easy to read, and interpret. All you need is a YouTube thumbnail maker to have a perfect thumbnail.

- **YouTube video thumbnail maker**

Knowing the importance of a remarkable, jaw-dropping thumbnail, you have now decided to figure it out, but you aren't a graphic designer or have zero knowledge of Photoshop. You can still make do with some tools while still having high-quality thumbnail. Here is a product for you!

- **Bannersnack**

This is a design tool used for thumbnail bomb creation. It's very easy to use as you can make a professional-looking and catchy thumbnail in little time without a graphic designer's experience. One amazing reason you should adopt Bannersnack is to stack layers in folds— a property needed for a top-notch thumbnail. Something must pop up at your viewers, and this layer property is the right match. In the Bannersnack, there are tons of icons and elements you can explore.

How to make a thumbnail for YouTube

Having discussed the inevitable nature of thumbnail and the usage of simple, flexible tools like a banner snack, you should be curious about how to make a thumbnail. Here, you are going to be creating your thumbnail in 5 easy steps. Sounds cool, right? Let go.

- **Use YouTube thumbnail's size.**

Having the right size thumbnail size is the most essential part of your design. You see people's word cut off, and images at random corners. That's an actual disaster. You don't want to make similar mistakes. Do you? The official size of the YouTube thumbnail size is 1280 pixel wide by 720pixel tall and a minimum width of 640pixel. You can optimize your thumbnail by leveraging on this size.

- **Selecting a background image**

After selecting the size, the next thing you want to do is choose a background image that would depict your content's visual presentation. Choose a picture of your own or a screenshot and upload it on bannersnack.

- **Type text to describe your video**

This is a very crucial area of your thumbs curation. Asides from your image displaying the content of your video, it's essential to tell your audience what your video conveys via text. You can use catchy phrases or the title of your video.

People are more likely to read the text on your thumbnail, than taking a step further to reading the text in the title of your video down below. Font placement would help a lot. Place your text in the negative space of your photo. If you don't have negative space, ensure to create some. Place an element in the background, play around with the opacity, and layer your text on top.

- **Decorate your thumbnail**

Here, your thumbnail's outlook will, to a considerable extent, depends on your creative prowess. You can play with color, text, and other features to develop a catchy jaw-dropping design. You can inscribe emoji to make your thumbnail look fun. In short, decorate your thumbnail as much as possible, but don't take away the image or text. It's imperative to state that you don't want to overwhelm your audience with so many things. So, play safe as much as you could.

- **Download your work**

After finishing the curation of your thumbnail, it's ripe for download! It's most common and advisable to download your work as a PNG file or a JPG. The choice is yours. Just ensure your file doesn't exceed 2MB. Tap on the green "Save" button in the top right corner, name, and save your work to your workspace, download, and finish.

Techniques to Drive Traffic to Your Youtube Channel You Must not Ignore

Without much ado, the following are ways you can keep your channel boozing with clicks and views;

- **Create top-notch content to get more YouTube views**

Serious-minded people won't take a chance in shunning channels they hitherto had viewed but with boring haggard content. For you to be able to retain your audience, you have to curate value-driven materials. The content type you will harness will depend on your business and audience target. The onus is finding a way of separating yourself from the pack. Why not hone your unique selling proposition and show it through video? Then incorporate some kind of content strategy tailored towards your YouTube channel. Identify what subject you would be relaying to your audience, draw a timeline, upload, and promote each video.

- **Upload frequently to get more traffic on YouTube.** When you upload more videos, you get more views, right? Well, that is valid to a large extent. Generally speaking, you want to upload more videos as much as possible while still maintaining the quality of your content. If you have the wherewithal in uploading multiple videos a week, please do. While at that, a decline in viewers will surge if you ever compromise the quality of your content. To make things look mature, it's safe for you to have a schedule. Determine whether you will be uploading once a week or twice a month and stick to it.

- **Edit your content to give quality**

To be candid, the top-notch video doesn't necessarily equate high-quality production. So, worry less if you don't have all the equipment to back your video strategy, especially if you are a starter. All you need is to make do with the resources you have and ensure your videos are professional. Ensure you take multiple recordings and dish out the best content to your audience.

- **Use tools to drive traffic to your channel**

Haven't you heard of TubeBuddy? A tool designed to manage some small tasks associated with a channel. TubeBuddy divides its tools into several strategies viz; productivity tools, video SEO tool, promotion tool, Data and research tool.

- **Engage others to increase traffic**

When you engage people genuinely, you are telling people that you have an interest in what they have to say. This can reinforce your popularity as other people can see your responses, suggestions, and comments. To explore this at its best, subscribe to other people's channels and include a link to a video of yours they might find valuable. Tell your users to drop comments and suggestions at the comment session after watching the video. This could further reinforce a sense of togetherness.

- **Look at live streaming**

Live streaming is unarguably one of the most popular ways to communicate. This isn't alien to YouTube. It allows you to connect with people real-time and perfect for spur-of-the-moment news.

- **Include an intro video to gain viewers and subscribers**

People don't observe what channel type they are when they watch your video. So, introduce yourself and let them know what is channel is all about to increase your traffic.

- **Give collaboration a chance**

You can explore the influencers to influence marketing your channel too. Look for someone who has already achieved it and ask the person to act as your brand evangelist. It might make a huge difference. Reach out to famous bloggers if they will like to feature your videos in a similar post or their social media network.

- **Promotion**

When it comes to YouTube, promotion is as important as production. Use every utilizable channel to promote your content. Social media, blogs, and websites are platforms you can explore. Create a blog post for your video and intimate your subscribers by sending them an email.

Other ways to drive traffic to your channel include;
● Getting inspiration from your favorite creators

- Optimize your channel
- Upload 360-degree video
- Use YouTube SEO

Techniques to take advantage of Youtube in the Business World

"We need to reposition our brand," "our website isn't attracting enough traffic," "we aren't strong enough to compete," are the common complaint by business owners. While a number of platforms are unique on their own, there is one avenue many brands aren't harnessing— YouTube. To many businesses, producing video content isn't something they find interesting hence, they fail to explore the opportunity it has to offer. At this global dispensation, the assemblage of your online presence must transcend the tentacles of Facebook and Twitter. This is an affirmation of the need to be strategic. You don't just post any content for the sake of posting. It's not going to add up. A thorough well thought out YouTube strategy would pay massively, a juicy dividend. You know making a video is possible right? What are the benefits you will get from YouTube? Posting on YouTube would boost your online presence.

YouTube belongs to Google. Ever wondered why the rate at which videos pop up in Google search results is on the rise? No, that's not a coincidence. The more you use YouTube, the more your chances of appearing on Google search results and subsequently increasing your ranking. As a business, you should be deliberate about maximizing your online presence, and an excellent way to go is YouTube since Google owns it.

- **YouTube will expose you to an enormous audience**

According to YouTube statistics;

- Over 30 million people visit YouTube daily watching over five million videos
- More than half of the viewers come from mobile devices, and these users watch a video with an average of 40minutes
- YouTube had a local version in more 88countries and 76 languages

After Google, YouTube is the second largest most popular search engine. YouTube is growing year in year out. The most striking advantage of YouTube is that it has a varied audience comprising people of different backgrounds. No matter what your brand is trying to promote, you can get the job done via YouTube.

- **Gained highly qualified traffic**

Your website might hit a few tons of million views, but if none of these viewers purchase your product, then what's the profit? YouTube can get you a sincere and loyal fan base who would patronize your business. You ensure you package yourself for your audience through several strategies. Think of giving your audience a free coupon after signing up with a link you show them in your presentation. You just attracted to yourself, email video viewers into email subscribers.

- **Utilize YouTube ad to reach a bigger audience**

The robust advertizing platform YouTube offers is something you would want to cash in on. There are Google Adwords, which is quite different from your paid advertisement. You know how many people are watching videos on YouTube. Think of serving your ads to qualified viewers who can turn to customers.

Amassing organically motivated traffic is very powerful, while paid traffic is a significant option too.

- **With video, people are bound to take action**
The need for a call-to-action (CTA) might not be alien to you on social media posts, blog posts, and a plethora of digital content. Content with CTA has shown that people take action than content without CTA.

Steps to Broadcasting Live and Its Benefit

Several benefits abound in video live streaming of events. In a wide variety of contexts, live video streaming can be impactful and efficient. Companies and businesses use live streaming to maximize effective direct communication with customers and community associates. Live streaming an event enables you to reach a more comprehensive degree of audience globally. While there are much importance of live streaming, setting up the equipment on your own requires some degree of expertise— technical skills. The following are the benefit of live streaming your events;

- **Large audience potential**

Physical events usually have a stretch limit. However, with live streaming, you can invite as many people as possible to attend your event. Physical events have inherited a backlog of loopholes. People often terminate gracing events to be held physically due to several factors—an astronomical rise in the cost of transportation, geographical divide, work commitment, and many others. The live stream has brought about the democratization of accessibility. All you need is to get your gadget charged, keep your Wi-Fi rolling, and sit within the comfort of your room or workplace to access information being disseminated.

- **Information with richer content**

Live streaming isn't limited to video and audio dissemination of events. You can infuse a survey of multimedia resources and tools to spice your content and get your audience more engaged. You even can access different methodologies for your presentation.

- **Ease of use and convenience**

While there are several myths on live streaming, many people nurse the assertion that live streaming is difficult to use. In actuality, it's not rocket science. All you need is a trustworthy streaming platform, your devices, a source of internet connection, and a conducive environment, and you are set to deliver your content.

- **Customer support**

It's quite challenging to resolve technical jargon without prior knowledge or experience of the problem at hand. Live streaming always comes with an assurance of having someone to support you if problems arise extempore. Google is the only solace for you provided that you are streaming on your own. If you are exploring a streaming platform, customer support will put you through in case of any challenges pops.

- **Mobile viewing**

A more significant percentage of audiences view video contents online via their mobile devices. You don't want to negotiate this advantage as you must keep with the trend and ensure your platform is mobile viewing enabled.

- **Affordability**

There are many video live streaming services, but these platforms have spams containing pops up. This could irritate your audience. Why not consider a professional streaming service. They are usually affordable.

Promoting Your Merchandize on YouTube Channel

The bottom line is that a range of strategies and approaches on how you can promote your merchandise exists. Every channel and subscriber base is unique in its niche. It's then safe to say there is no absolute 'how-to' you can point at that simplify the way forward. While there isn't any concrete answer, this gives a chance to uncertainty, and you don't want to operate base on trial and error. That isn't the smartest decision to take.

Despite all odds, there are still several questions you can ask while trying to fix ways of promoting your merchandise on your channel.

- **Is your audience engaged?**

You can have a pool of audiences spanning from several thousand to a few million. This colossal traffic isn't as relevant as how engaged are your audience. If there is little or no synergy between your content and your audience, you are in bad shape. You must device compelling strategies to get your audience clicking those like buttons, eager to comment, feedback, and much robust interaction.

- **How competitive and robust is your brand?**

There are tons of people selling your product. There are many people whose selling strategies and approaches to market are top-notch. This isn't an attempt to create fear or to be discouraged. The question is what you would do to have that competitive advantage that can stretch your brand off the bottom line. The answer to this daunting challenge would be to what extent is your brand unique? How secure is your brand? Do a quick analysis of the search activity related to your brand. This will allow you to reconcile with all odds and give you a safe pad to launch.

- **What do you think merchandise can do for you?**

In the grand scheme of things, it's quite imperative to do a quick assessment of yourself. In trying to figure out, you ask several questions. What do you want from your constant efforts? Is it some side money to level up your pocket, personal awareness, self-pride, or an admixture of the trio? Knowing what you expect from your merchandise and setting your goals will guide your decision to start selling and promoting.

Chapter 3

TIPS TO BE CONSISTENT ON YOUTUBE

Consistency, they say, can break the most inaccessible of rock. You're only consistent in things that you have a great interest in. Such things matter to you. Uploading videos consistently on YouTube shows that you take it seriously as a job. Being a YouTuber is a full-time job, and it is gratifying. But, when you upload one video today and don't come up with another exciting video till two months, you will lose subscribers to other channels. Being consistent uploading contents implies you are a dedicated person. So, to maintain your followers, you should be consistent with uploading your video on YouTube. Consistency gives your followers, subscribers & audience a reason to be anticipating your next video. If you're a consistent YouTuber, your audience should know what they will be getting. This doesn't mean that your subscribers will know the nitty-gritty of how your whole video is going to be, but they'll have expectations of the specific people's quality, style, humor, information, etc. that your content will provide. Here are tips to help you stay consistent uploading videos on YouTube;

Plan your time appropriately: Planning is vital to stay consistent in anything you do. Planning your time will help define your purpose, especially if you have other commitments. Set aside days to schedule your video, days for shooting, days for editing, and days for uploading. That way, you can remember what you've done and what you're yet to do. Do not deviate from your schedule.

Show your video schedule on your YouTube channel banner: One right way to ensure that you stick to your plan & get things done faster and easier is to have your schedule shown on your Channel banner. This means showing your followers what day(s) & possibly even what time you'll upload another video to your channel. This set of clear deadlines gives you extra motivation to get your content out & available in time.

Produce videos in batches: You can strive to produce videos in batches. This will enable you relax while releasing your video at intervals. Let's say you plan to release two videos a week. You can batch shoot eight videos at a time.

Make a checklist when necessary: the checklist is another way to stay on track. You can make a checklist of the equipment you will need, how to edit, and how and when to shoot your video, etc.

Have a unique and consistent thumbnail pattern: This way. Your audience can easily recognize your content when it shows up on their feed. This will increase your channel's click-through-rate (CTR), and YouTube can start pushing your video to more viewers.

Know your audience and represent them: to be able to produce quality content that'll attract views, you have to know who you're making the video for. If your audiences are mainly adolescents between 13 to 15 years of age, you won't get patronage if you're creating content that adults can only understand. If your audiences are mainly women, you'll do well to address them like " hi ladies" and not " hey guys."

Find your specific niche: your niche should be unique and target something that, even if it is common, will be beneficial to the audience. If you are clothes reviewers, it won't seem well you review a machine tomorrow unless it is used to make clothes.

YouTube Videos - Quality or Quantity

Let us get one thing right: just because you spent a lot of time doing something, doesn't mean your result is any higher or better quality.

One sure way to get more viewers and growing your YouTube channel is by making videos on things that people are seriously searching for. Everyone has one or two problems to solve. It becomes a relief seeing the light at the end of the tunnel, by finally getting solutions to our problems. Let's say I just purchased a personal computer, which is overheating. I want to fix this problem. So I went to Google and searched, " how can I fix my PC's overheating?. Before I knew it, I landed on YouTube and watched a video of a YouTuber on how he solved this problem. I applied his method, and the result was perfect. Now tell me, if I have a similar problem in the future, whose channel will i go first?. Well, your guess is as good as mine. That's quality. He delivers quality content on his platform. Quality, but very short, videos that solve people's problems will endear them to your channel.

In another light, you should also strive to upload videos as often as possible to maintain your video's consistency. Your channel should not be scanty all because you're trying to prioritize quality. It all boils down to balancing the two extremes.

Sometimes to achieve the most views and overall growth, you have to get your video out there to gather more views. If you can get it done quickly with your video being the right quality, then post it. If it's not of the right quality, then try and put some more time into making it the right quality.

Steps to Creating a YouTube AdSense Account

Creating a YouTube AdSense account is the way toward monetizing your YouTube video. Doing this the wrong way means you are jeopardizing your chance of making money on YouTube. Find below some more accessible way to create YouTube AdSense account;

- Go to YouTube.
- Click on your profile and click on YouTube studio.
- You will get a prompt to open your channel dashboard. From here, you click on monetize-

tion. Note: You will only be able to apply for monetization when your channel has crossed 1000 subscribers and a 4000hours video view.
- Click on the 'apply now' icon on your YouTube dashboard.
- A prompt displaying some list of essential steps you must complete is displayed.

Step one - Review partner program: Read and agree to the YouTube partner program. This is the agreement that makes it possible for you to start earning money on YouTube.

Step two – sign up for Google AdSense Account: You need an AdSense account to monetize your channel and start making money. Click on the start and answer some questions that will be prompted.

You will be asked if you have an existing AdSense account. Please say yes if you have it. Approving a new Adsense account can take up to 1 month. If you click No, you will be directed to create a Google AdSense account. Click continue to proceed.

You will be directed to your email and select your Google account, which you wish to create your Google AdSense with.

Choose your country and agree to terms and conditions.

You will be taken to the payment address detail where you are expected to fill in your names, email address, house address, phone number, and specific customer information.

Your login pin will be sent to your email to make money through Western Union bank transfer.

Click on the submit icon.

You will be redirected to your host where you can start using AdSense. If you are not automatically redirected within a few seconds, click on the redirect icon yourself.

Step three - This is the stage where YouTube will review your channel to make sure it complies with the YouTube monetization policy. YouTube will usually email you a decision within one month.

YouTube Best Practices

Best practices are a set of professional conducts that are agreed on and accepted as being correct. That said, YouTube is not just any space where you dump videos and leave. You must conduct yourself properly because your brand's growth is a function of how well you conform to rules and guidelines from YouTube and other respected individuals on the platform. The tips below will guide you towards conforming to YouTube codes and order;

Inform your audience when you want to take a leave of absence from your page: along the line, you might get busy and want to concentrate on other things going on in your life. It is only desirable you tell your subscribers that you will be off your page for some time. If possible, tell them the time frame that the leave will end. Let them know when you are likely to come back fully. That way, they will keep anticipating if you were giving them quality content before.

Maximize the search engine optimization(SEO): The search engine optimization holds great importance to ensure your content are reached by the vast majority of audiences who are populating YouTube in search of knowledge, idea and some fun moments. To get this, you should understand the importance of having searchable keywords in your 'about video' section.

Give a proper title and description for your video: The title gives your viewers a little idea of what the video is about. The best practice here is to use a catchy description and title. A lot more information about yourself or the video can be added in the description section.

Engage your audience often: YouTube is more than just a platform for uploading videos. You can build an exciting connection with your followers through a series of interactive video sessions.

Create shorter length videos: Videos under 2minutes duration get the most views.

Tips to make YouTube Videos go Viral Most YouTubers are not using

For a platform that has 300hours of video upload every minute, the fact is YouTube is already going viral. Your job is to create your content and have it among the most trended YouTube videos. If you like to get your YouTube video go viral, then let get you started.

Do your job well by using searchable keywords in your video description: Users with SEO standard keywords get higher views than those who don't understand this search optimization technique. The beauty of the search optimization is that it helps, naturally, to make your video go viral. The SEO algorithm is designed to search related keywords within some identified video niche. Through this, it brings video that complies with standard into the top of the search when users search any items on YouTube or even Google with the same keywords as your video. You have to do your job by adding such keywords into the context of the content surrounding the video.

Use proper video name: You can't upload a video you made about 'how to write a novel' with names such as 'vytri.mkv.' You can rename this as 'video on novel writing.' That works better.

Err on the side of making shorter videos rather than longer ones: Shorter duration videos get higher view because many people are interested in shorter duration videos tailored to address their needs. The more views a video gets, the more it trends and goes viral.

Engage overlays when necessary: Overlays are those small boxes of text that pop up when a viewer is watching a video on YouTube. The text can come as a clickable link that works wonders with a strong call to actions (CTAs) for your viewers, whether through subscribing to your channel, making some purchases, or even staying more than necessary, viewing more info on your channel. Don't forget to also put the call to actions (CTAs) in the video description box so that there is a repetition of what action you're calling the audience to take.

Let your video provide value: it is not just about uploading videos on YouTube for the sake of it. Is your video delivering the right benefits? When you make sure every single post of yours is trying to tell and teach people what they don't know, you are assured of getting waves of likes, comments, and shares coming your way.

Tell some stories with your video: people like to watch relatable videos telling a story they can relate to. Use your video to achieve this and watch it go viral.

Don't let criticism gets to you and discourage you: Most times, when your video goes viral, people will most likely have one or two things to say about it, whether good or bad. Seeing some of the negative comments can discourage you from trying again. Don't be discouraged. Let every criticism serves as a means of encouragement to you.

Setting up a YouTube channel for success: Things to take note of

YouTube is one of the vastly risen platforms in the world, perhaps the most sought after video platforms for entrepreneurs, tech experts, teachers, and students. These categories of users have enjoyed the platforms over time as a means for learning and disseminating information. One specific area of concern, as far as this book is concerned, is for those that use YouTube for business to make money. It is unarguable that many people have not understood the simple ways to set up their YouTube channel to attract viewers as well as to gain more income. If you have been considering setting up a YouTube channel for your business or creating awareness and teaching others, but you have not been making success, find this book as your most significant investment. Want to build a successful YouTube channel? Then come right here. Here, I am going to show you some efficient strategies to create a successful YouTube page that thrives.

1. **Define your audience**: The first step in getting things right is targeting your audience and tailor your content to meet their needs specifically. Are you making content for kids, adolescents, adults, or aged people? Are you creating a country's specific content – your target might be North America or South America? To better address this, consider the following tips;

What problem does your targeted audience want to solve: Are your audience interested in finding videos to help them make money online? Are they interested in fixing some issues affecting their phones? Or they are probably interested in checking phone reviews before they decide on getting one? All of these are questions you should consider asking yourself. Find a right niche for your content. Make sure your chosen niche is the one you are very good at.

In what form does your audience want your content: You have to make sure the content you are choosing is teachable with videos, because not all materials can work well with videos. Videos are particularly suitable for; product reviews, educational purposes, cooking tutorials, demonstrations of all sorts, etc.

2. **Make attractive videos**: one common way to get views on YouTube is to modify your video to be able to rank high in YouTube's searches without necessarily having to put much effort. But this method might just serve you temporarily. There are organic ways to create videos people want to watch, and that people will watch.

- You must understand, genuinely, why people watch the video they watch. People watch videos to learn how to solve their problems and to entertain themselves. Your video must be tailored to either of these two options. A super long story doesn't really address your viewer's problem. Too long introduction doesn't pass your message across. People want concise videos tailored to solve their problems, not a TV show.

- Prioritize quality over quantity while deciding your videos: people are not particularly interested in how long your video is. They are more interested in content over quantity. High-quality videos rate higher attract viewer's attention.
- Make a name for yourself and be consistent: Your YouTube is not something you set up for the sake of doing so. It is something you should invest your time in. Professionalism is one of the secrets of a successful YouTuber.

3. **Optimize your videos to be searchable**: You will prefer your video to come as a first priority whenever anyone searches any content within your niche on YouTube or Google. This is where search engine optimization (SEO) comes in. Videos sometimes show up as a search result on Google, which can drive a sizeable number of views to your channel. The key to this is uploading your videos with keywords that people are searching for the most. Keywords like

'how-to,' and 'what is' usually rate high. There are two essential parts of YouTube optimization that you need to cater for most. These include;

- **Let your video be relevant to a search**: YouTube algorithm is designed such that it brings videos that are relevant to people's search on the search engine. It looks for these keywords in your titles, video description, and tag. Look at the image and notice the use of the keyword in titles, descriptions, and tags. Notice the repetitive usage of the keyword 'tutorial.'

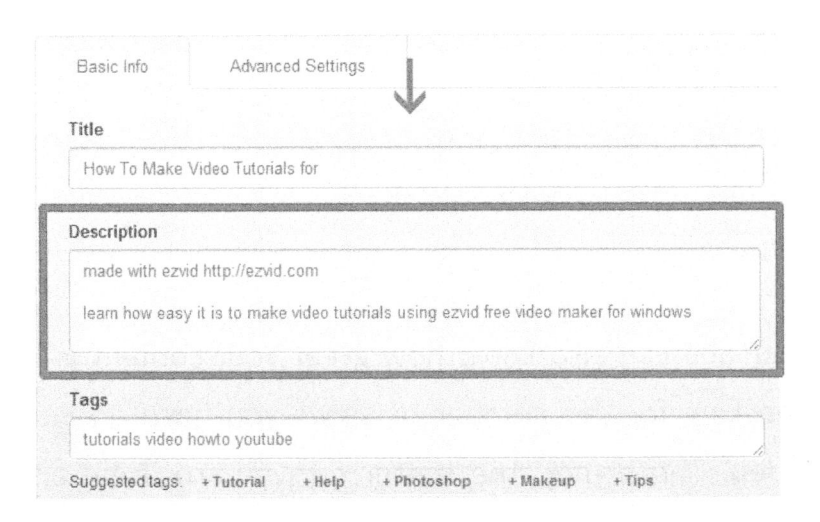

Basic Info	Advanced Settings

Title

How To Make Video Tutorials for

Description

made with ezvid http://ezvid.com

learn how easy it is to make video tutorials using ezvid free video maker for windows

Tags

tutorials video howto youtube

Suggested tags: + Tutorial + Help + Photoshop + Makeup + Tips

Maximize the use of viewers' engagements and comments: YouTube algorithm also considers this while ranking your video. The algorithm checks what length of the video your viewers started losing interest only to stop watching. It is okay if about 60% - 70% of your users are viewing the complete video. The graph below shows that about 60%of his viewers watched the full video.

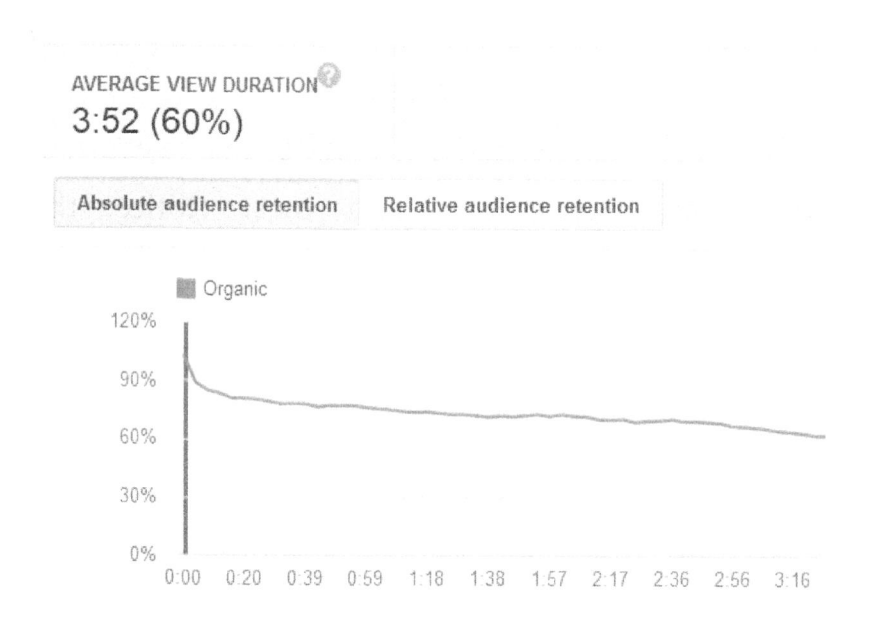

AVERAGE VIEW DURATION
3:52 (60%)

| Absolute audience retention | Relative audience retention |

Organic

YouTube can also know how great your content is by checking for the number of views you have on your video. The higher, the better for you. YouTube also checks the ratio of thumbs up to thumbs down. Thumbs ups are great, the higher, the better for you. The number of shares on your video are equally important. YouTube understands that people will ordinarily share great content. The higher the number of shares, the better.

Let's further take a look at how to market your channel to get more subscribers;

Maximize the use of call-to-action (CTAs) to get more subscribers on your platform: You have already delivered excellent content for your viewers. But you want them to click the subscribe button to see more of your videos. How do you do it? Well, you have to tell them. Look at the image below. The YouTuber makes use of a subscribe caption at the end of his video to call viewers' attention to subscribe to his channel.

Put your website's link somewhere in the video descrption: This might be necessary to direct people to your site. See below as an example.

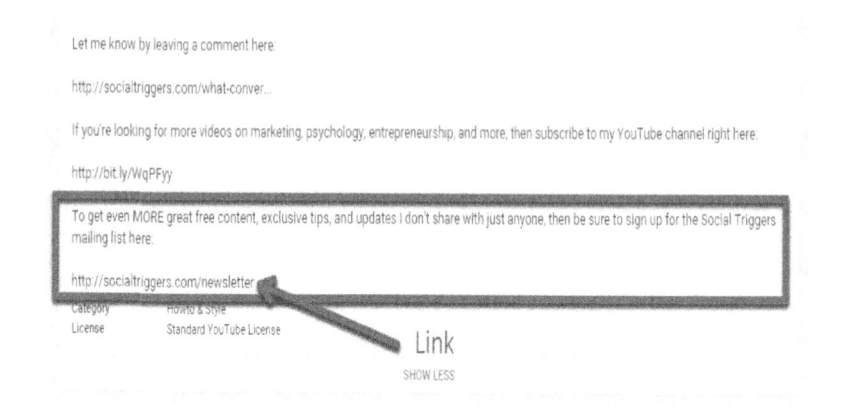

Note: Remember that while growing in this terrain, you will receive a lot of comments ranging from bad, worse, and enjoyable. You should not let them get to you. Instead, you should use them as an opportunity to improve.

YouTube Video Ideas and Crucial Things You Need to Know

If you are a beginner in the YouTube space, and you don't have any idea of what video you can create for a start, here is a list you can select from.

Do it yourself videos: You can work around making some videos to teach people how to do some specific things on their own—things like craftworks.

How-to videos: This is one of the most search terms on YouTube space. People are interested in knowing how to sing, dance, play guitar, play games, etc. The list in this category is not exhaustible.

Cooking tutorials: You can start sharing your favorite cooking tips and recipe.

Product reviewing: You can create a YouTube space and be reviewing phones. Telling people about the specifications of phones, and where one phone is preferable to the other.

Infographics analysis: People love statistical information detailed and explained with attractive charts.

Talk about some myths: Are there some things that you know as myths? You can talk about them so that people can understand it too.

Music videos: Bring friendly music content for your viewers.

Comedy: This might even make you go viral.

Unboxing videos: Make videos unboxing some latest gadgets and technologies.

Favorite Apps, favorite games, and favorite sports videos.

Chapter 4

STEPS TO SHOOT A GOOD YOUTUBE VIDEO

Today, in 2020, it appears no online platform has ever created wealth and learning opportunities like YouTube. Due to the fast-growing demand for YouTube's market, the need to learn how to shoot a YouTube video like a professional becomes necessary. There may be thousands of people out there, creating the same content just like you on YouTube. But one thing makes a difference: your ability to shoot quality and excellent YouTube video and of course, nothing comes easy. You have to put in the right amount of dedication to learn the perfect way of getting your video out there. This is necessary to make your video unique.

You might want to consider the following strategies to shoot your YouTube video;

1. **Plan your video:** You can barely have any flint of success in something you don't plan for. Successful people understand the importance of planning and can go the extra length to invest their time into an efficient planning strategy. You have to know why you are creating a YouTube video in the first place. Who are your targeted audiences? Do you want to create awareness about a product? Or you probably want to

make a fun video to get likes, comments, and attention from viewers. All of these must be accurately mapped out and answered before you get your video out there. Let me give you some hints to know how you can better plan your video as a beginner.

a. **Engage YouTube SEO:** Some keywords can be added to your video description to make it more searchable on YouTube. This is so that when people search for a particular video online, your content will come up at the top. See, the game here is that people are very much likely to check out the content that appears first. They believe that for it to appear first, then it must be the right content they're looking for. To do this effectively, you can search for people doing the same thing you want to do. Check their videos by entering a specific search term, and confirm the traffic on their video. If they have more traffic than others within the same niche, they may have the right content and maximize their SEO effectively. You can equally make your content searchable by following their pattern and creating a great YouTube content.

b. **Search for a good location for your video:** you can always set up your camera in various places to find the perfect physical spot for your video; as you preview options, consider what's in the background of the video and the lighting condition to explore the best location.

2. **Have the right equipment ready:** You have never probably seen a successful farmer without his farm tool. Never have you seen a school teacher writing with his teeth. Thinking of creating YouTube without a camera is obviously like a kite that has holes even before being cast. That idea is not going to work. The following are essential materials you'd need to create a quality YouTube video;

a. **Camera**: Something as simple as your phone camera can get the job done most time if you know how to use it. With the right camera, even a gorilla will look more like a prince charming. Investing in a good camera to shoot your video is a priority.

b. **Microphone**: If you created an excellent content, but people cannot hear you all because of an inaudible speaker or receiver, it is as good as not creating any video at all.

c. **Proper lightning**: Cameras don't work well without a good light source. You should always endeavor to shoot your video using the right light source.

d. **Video editing software**: There are many video editing software out there to give your video the perfect appearance. There are now YouTube video editors that you can contract to help you. This even creates jobs for video editors who know how to do their job effectively.

3. **Prepare the appropriate stage for your video:** You can't be teaching your audience how to prepare a particular food, only for you to be displaying pictures of wild animals or jungle as your background. Your video stage must reflect what you are talking about in the video. This is where setting the right stage comes in. Don't forget to clear all the specks of dirt behind you while making your video.

4. **Be confident while using the camera:** I was once disappointed when I watched a video where the maker could not even look at the camera in the face. Only to discover later that it was his first video. Thing is it does not matter if it is your first or not — since you

don't know who might watch in the long run, you have to put in your best appearance.

5. **Start recording:** having ticked all required boxes, and getting your confidence surged through your sleeve, the next is to start recording your video. Let me add one or two advice here;

a. while recording your video, ensure you consider the camera in your front as an audience. That way, you will be able to relate better.

b. Also, don't get panicked about making mistakes in your video. We all make mistakes, don't we?. If you made an error saying what you are not supposed to say, just calm down and continue recording. You don't have to repeat your statement to make it accurate. You can always edit the video when you finished.

6. **Start editing your video:** here comes another big chance to give your video that perfect aesthetic you can provide it. There are many premium software you can invest in. Some YouTubers don't do this by themselves; they hire a video editor and pay. Video editors are professionals, and they help you perfect your video in a way to give the audience the appeals they want. If you make some mistakes in your video,

this is where you can correct it. There are varieties of video editing software available for download on your Mac or PC, such as Adobe Premier Pro, Final cut X, Filmora, Movavi, etc. Your job is to find the right one for you. You might as well consider customer reviews on each software to inform your choice better.

YouTube Video structure

From research, about 300hours of videos are being uploaded on YouTube every minute, and around 5billion YouTube videos are being watched every month. This statistics is not to scare you. It is for you to know about the competition ahead. The technological wake of the 21st century has given people enough access to information. For a platform like YouTube where people are cashing out daily – depending on how great your contents are - you can expect more significant competition. But you can do better, can't you? This is why your YouTube space must have a workable structure to address your growing audience better.

Let us take a look at why structuring your video is very important, to begin with;

- **Getting more views**: The YouTube algorithm is designed such that the more views you get per video, the more you are ranked. The more the youtube ranking, the more searchable your content becomes.

- **Builds brand through familiarity and consistency**: Getting a workable structure for your video gives you a loyal fan base. This is because your followers are already familiar with your content. They already know where to go if they want to watch that type of video next time. For example, if you have a niche in comedy and at the same time in technology, this is not being consistent, and you should try and avoid it if you can.

Structuring your video

A good YouTube video structure takes viewers from the start to the end and gets them hooked coming for more. The following tips are handy while structuring your video;

1. **Make a short introduction of your video first**: Getting people aware, albeit briefly, of what they are about to watch will go a long way towards getting them started with your video. Tell viewers what you are about to show them how it is going to solve their

problems and why they should watch the video, you give them a reason not to browse away from your video. Always remember you have about 10 seconds to convince your audience and get their attention.

Pro tip: **do not give away all the information in the introduction. If you do, you give them no reason to stay again because they've seen it all.**

2. **Developing the key content of the video:** When you have already gotten your viewers' attention, the next thing is to intimate them about the great content you have prepared for them. You can navigate the steps below for proper direction;

a. **Bear in mind that people always have problems to solve, so you have to tell them about the problem:** Use about 2.5minutes of the video to discuss the difficulties your video can solve. Do you want to tell them how to fix a particular software or hardware component on their PC? Are you interested in getting them aware of how to solve a related maths problem? All of these must be appropriately discussed in this part of the video.

Pro tip: While discussing the problem, try to show concerns as much as possible. They feel relaxed getting to know many people have been in their shoes before, and they were able to scale through.

b. **Offer solutions to their problems:** You can use about 4minutes here to discuss solutions to their problems. Tell them precisely what method to be adopted in solving their problems. Relate the answers with vivid and practical examples of how they work.

c. **Hook them further:** It is not just about discussing solutions to their problems, it is more of getting them glued from the first second to the last second of your video. This is where the hook comes in. Sometimes, people get bored quickly, and you can try to throw some funny statements in between to bring them back.

3. **Engage your audience:** It is not enough to solve your audience's problem; it is as well good to engage your audience. Ask your audience questions. Let them tell you how they feel. You can even tell them when next to expect another video from you. This way, you create a good relationship with them.

YouTube Video Editing Tips and Tricks

Editing is the last process involved in getting your YouTube video out there for public consumption. This step, if gotten wrong, can jeopardize the whole process. That is why you need to do a great job while editing your video. The following are necessary tips to edit your video like a professional;

1. **Create a record of your raw video footage, sounds, and other documents**: Of course, you understand that having a messy worktable is terrible if you want the finest of what you do. You should create a folder on your computer where you can store video before editing, audios, and videos after editing. This way, you will know where to search for any important file or video.

2. **Select the video editing software that you can best work with:** You don't necessarily need to invest millions of dollars before you have a perfect video editing tool that can give you what you want. You must invest in a good video editing software that can enable you to upload your videos to YouTube within a few minutes. One popular video editing software in

the market, which has been trusted over time by video professionals, is the *Screencast-o-Matic video editor*. It has easy-to-use tools that can improve your video appearance within seconds to minutes.

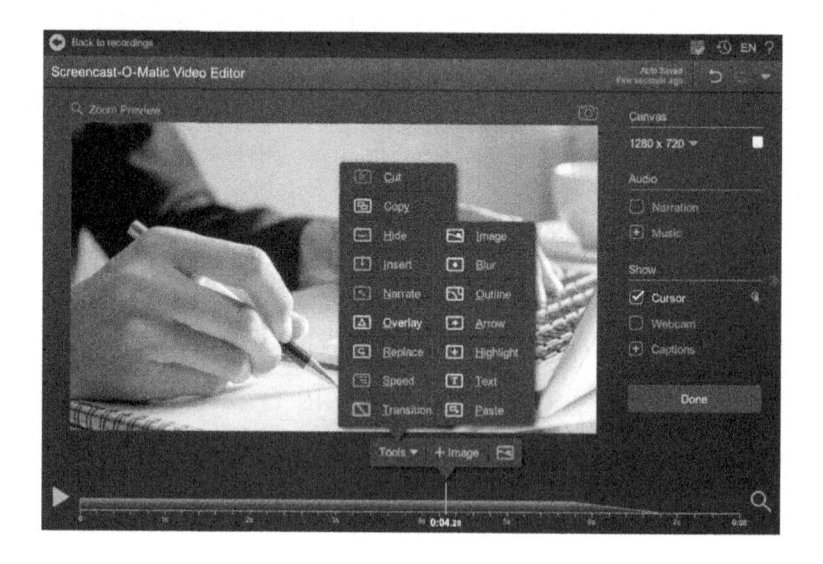

Screencast-o-matic video editor

Editing your videos can be done in three parts.

- **Assembling your video and recordings**: Join all the videos on your phone, camera, and computers together on a single file for easy upload into the editing software.

- **Add more sauce to your video by adding texts, images, and more:** Adding texts and pictures to your videos with the *Screencast-o-Matic video editor* is very easy. To add pictures, scroll to the spot on your timeline where you want to add your photo. Tap on the Tools menu and go to 'Overlay.' And select 'images' from a list of options.

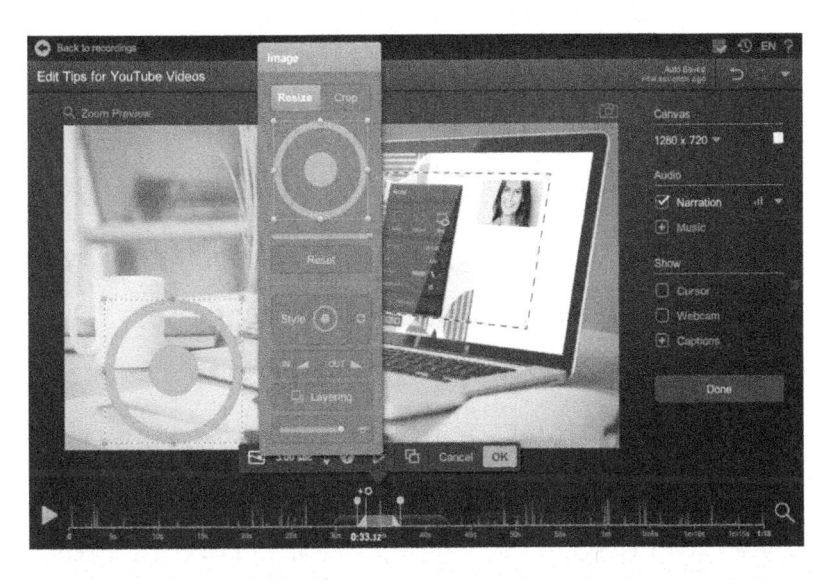

Adding texts to your video

3. **Go live!** This is the next step of your video editing, and the last step where you can get to upload your readymade video on the YouTube platform.

The right ways to Upload Your Videos to YouTube

The moment you finish giving your video the right editing, what is next is how to get it to YouTube – going live!. But before you think of uploading your video on YouTube, consider the following tips;

- **Ensure the video file you are sending to YouTube is a supported format:** YouTube supports many video file formats, ranging from MOV, MPEG4, MP4, AVI, WMV, MPEG-PS, FLV, 3GPP, WebM, DNxHR, Prores, CineForm, HEVC (h265). If your video is not in any of these formats, do well to convert it.

- **You can add sounds to your video right after uploading:** If you have not yet decided on which audio you want to add to your video, you are still safe. You can add the sound from the YouTube collection. YouTube has many selections of audio in its library.

There are two ways to upload your videos on YouTube;

1. Through your YouTube account
2. Using Screencast-O-Matic's video platform.

Uploading a video to YouTube Using YouTube Account

YouTube account can be used to upload your edited video on YouTube for viewing by your followers. Take the following steps to upload using your YouTube account;

1. Login to your YouTube account
2. Tap the video icon at the top right-hand side of the window, which is usually found next to the user icon.
3. Tap the 'upload video' icon.
4. Then, click 'Selected files to upload' to find the saved video file on your computer or Mac. Or, you can even drag the video from your computer and drop it into the window.
5. Engage the search engine optimization by adding an SEO friendly title so that viewers can quickly discover your video via search engines. Giving your video the right keywords will increase its discoverability in any search engine – be it Google or YouTube inbuilt search.

6. Add a video description so viewers can get the idea of what they are about to watch.

Tricks to Uploading YouTube videos through Screencast-O-Matic's Video platform

1. Click on the '+' icon next to the options menu in the YouTube account.
2. Select the 'upload to YouTube icon.' A popup will be displayed where you can launch the web browser.
3. Enter your account and 'Allow' Screencast-O-Matic to gain access to your YouTube Google Account.
4. After setting up, you can easily use the Screencast-O-Matic to upload by clicking on the 'upload to YouTube' icon.

Tips for Maintaining YouTube followership

Maintaining a strong follower base on YouTube is one sure way you can get a high number of views for your content. That said, there are tips to enable you to grow followers in large numbers on YouTube. You can find the following tips useful;

1. **Build your video keyword around the most searched keyword in the niche you are targeting**: Try to research the most searched keyword for the video you want to upload on YouTube. You can watch videos of people who are in the same niche on YouTube and are getting more views. Check how they structure their keyword. If possible, try and build your keyword before you even start making videos. This will help you to develop content that is centered on that keyword eventually.

2. **Build a community with your audience**: Some YouTubers just upload videos and leave the platform without regard to their subscribers. Don't do that. Find a way to actively interact with your followers through opening the comment box, likes, and dislikes button. You can even reply to their comment. That way, they will know you have their best interest at heart.

3. **Let your channel be appealing**: Appearance matters. Let your channel look professional to attract viewers. Branding your YouTube channel might be the journey you will take to get more subscribers on your channel.

4. **Advertise your YouTube video on some other social media spaces**: You can share your YouTube video link on your Instagram, Facebook, LinkedIn, and Twitter. That way, you can have many of your friends visiting your platform to watch your content and subscribe to your channel.

5. **Increase your presence by uploading videos of you sometimes**: This way, your subscribers can easily relate with you.

6. **Post catchy titles and thumbnails to have a higher click-through-rate (CTR):** This makes your video ranks higher.

7. **Utilize YouTube cards**: YouTube card provides an avenue to add more videos to your videos. This way, viewers can stay longer on your channel, trying to check out the next content. Even if they don't finally click the video, their prolonged staying will increase your YouTube channel ranking.

8. **Increase your uploading rate**: Frequent uploading of videos on your channel will tell viewers that you're consistent. This way, they can keep coming to your channel.

Ads for Monetizing YouTube Channel

YouTube pays you money for letting other YouTubers run their ads on your video. The following tips are essential if you want to monetize YouTube ads;

1. **Getting started**: Visit the YouTube official advertising page and click "get started." This prepares you on the track to launch your ad campaign.

a. Select which videos you want to promote by copying the video URL to your YouTube video.

b. Fill in the information needed to complete your ad, including the headline and two lines of description, and choose a thumbnail. As you enter your information, you can see a preview of how your video will look.

c. Indicate where you want to send the traffic when viewers click on the video or ads. Here, you can select your website or your YouTube channel.

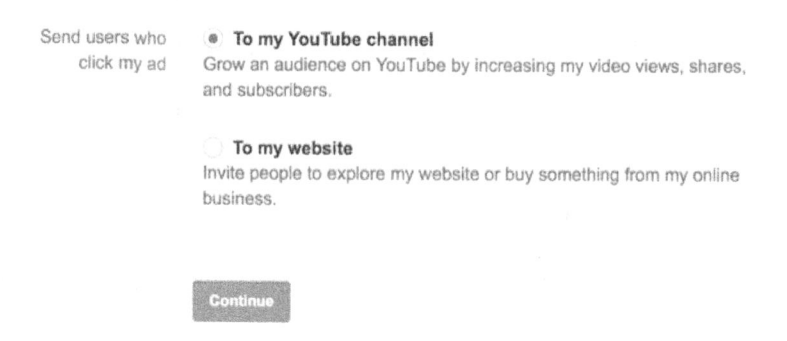

- **To my YouTube channel**: Grow an audience on YouTube by increasing my video views, shares, and subscribers.
- **To my website**: Invite people to explore my website or buy something from my online business.

d. Select the maximum cost per view (CPV). This is so that you won't be paying YouTube more than the revenue a view is giving you.

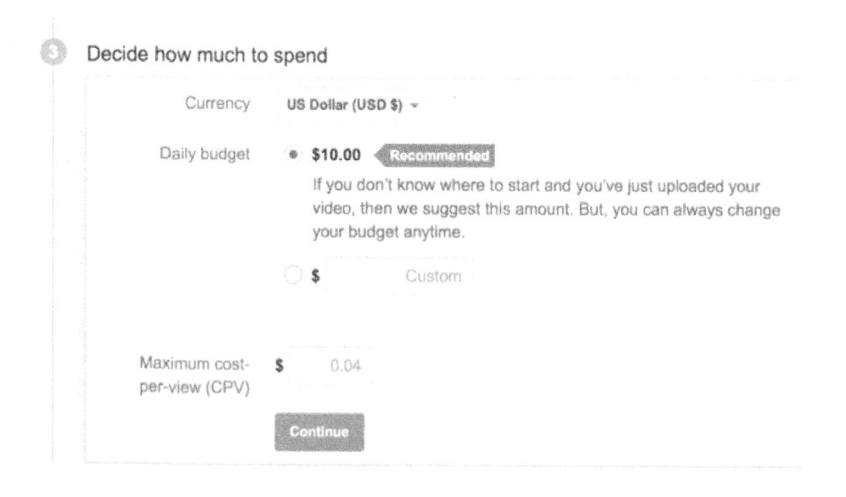

Decide how much to spend

- Currency: US Dollar (USD $)
- Daily budget: $10.00 (Recommended) — If you don't know where to start and you've just uploaded your video, then we suggest this amount. But, you can always change your budget anytime.
- Maximum cost-per-view (CPV): $0.04

e. **Select your audience:** you may like to restrict your content from being seen by some specific class.

Choose a target audience (optional)

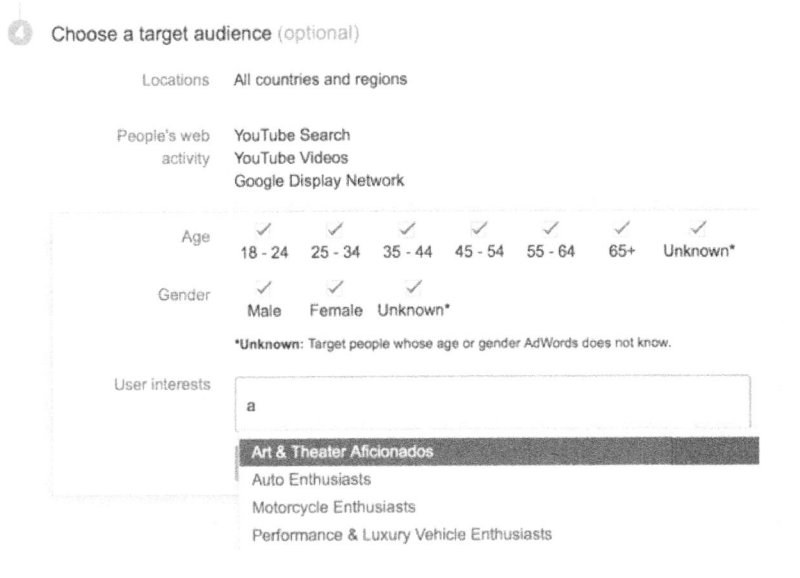

Locations	All countries and regions
People's web activity	YouTube Search YouTube Videos Google Display Network
Age	✓ 18-24 ✓ 25-34 ✓ 35-44 ✓ 45-54 ✓ 55-64 ✓ 65+ ✓ Unknown*
Gender	✓ Male ✓ Female ✓ Unknown*

*Unknown: Target people whose age or gender AdWords does not know.

User interests

a

Art & Theater Aficionados
Auto Enthusiasts
Motorcycle Enthusiasts
Performance & Luxury Vehicle Enthusiasts

2. Generating revenue using ads

YouTube can play ads on your video. That way, you can start making money

● Click on your profile picture at the top right-hand corner of your YouTube account.

● Tap on 'creator studio.'

● Scroll down to the bottom and select monetization.

● Tap enable monetization to enable your video for monetization,

Monetization

Account Status

You have disabled ads on all videos where you own the rights.

Enable monetization

- Agree to YouTube terms and agreements and select what type of ads you want to allow.

- Link your YouTube to your Google AdSense account and tap on the monetization bar, followed by clicking on the 'learn more.'

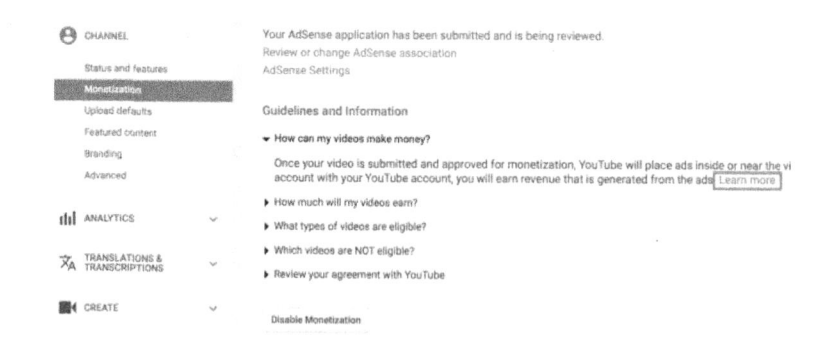

- Sign in to AdSense or create another if you don't have already, and select the language. Then set it up finally. Await notifications confirming success in your email.

About the Author

Anthony Henderson is a professional YouTuber with over 10 years of expertise delivering content on YouTube. He has a YouTube space where he tutors and guides followers about new YouTube trends and technologies. He is an animal lover, and loves watching football at leisure.

Anthony had an MBA from Cornell University, Ithaca USA. He is married with two beautiful kids.

Made in the USA
Monee, IL
19 October 2021